ANF
011.73
ANDE

50 BOOKS TO READ IF YOU'RE...
AN ARMCHAIR
DETECTIVE

ERIC KARL ANDERSON

murdoch books

Sydney | London

COSY CRIME
AND THE THRILL
OF THE CHASE

Is there anything better than cosying up late at night and getting lost in a great mystery? A country house, a perplexing crime, a circle of suspects, a cunning detective, red herrings, a shocking twist... These elements make up most of the exhilarating mysteries we love. Yet there are myriad variations and strategies writers use to chill, surprise and delight us. Those who have been captivated by such stories will want to know what to read next. These are my suggestions.

Some of the titles herein are considered supreme examples of the genre. Some are newer or less well known. Some veer more towards crime, comedy, the supernatural or the literary. They vary from classics to bestsellers to the more obscure and far-reaching. My intention is to offer a wide variety so that you can discover some new-to-you great mysteries.

Hark back to a nineteenth-century tome considered to be a pivotal tale of mystery or explore an array of choices from the golden age of detective fiction. Meet super-sleuths who are charming or pompous. Find out how mysteries incorporate and respond to wider social and political changes. Discover newer writers who are reinventing what the detective story can do. From lavish English mansions to small-town America, from a train journey in the Andes to a bustling community in Botswana, and a Japanese island, the settings of these tales circle the globe and present a wide diversity of characters.

Of course, this list isn't completely comprehensive. It has been designed to hint at possibilities and suggest authors you might want to try. The great thing about mysteries is that if you like a particular one, there's usually an entire series of books featuring the same detective or location. Each book offers its own unique style and form of suspense. For all the varieties of fiction listed in this book, I hope they are all mysteries that any lover of the genre will enjoy and savour.

Challenge yourself to solve the crime before the culprit is revealed. Take this list as a reading guide with titles to tick off one at a time, or pick and choose from the books within to try something new. The choice is yours, and the game is afoot!

NB The publication dates throughout apply to the year of first publication in the country of origin. Where several translations of a book exist, I have selected the one I'm most familiar with.

FIONA BARTON * 2016

When a high-profile trial involves a man accused of a terrible crime, he usually gives a statement to the media where the public hangs upon his every word. This original novel looks past the man to the woman often standing silently behind him. What would happen if we heard her story?

This thrilling novel begins with the recent accidental death of Glen Taylor, the primary suspect in a long-running investigation concerning a missing girl. Now the police and journalists turn to Jean, his quiet and submissive wife who always stood behind him. Investigative reporter Kate Waters is determined to get her full story. As Jean's version of events is revealed and she moves into the spotlight, we discover what this enigmatic widow really knows and why the truth is sometimes too difficult to face.

Before writing this debut novel, Fiona Barton was a journalist, which has provided her with a special insight into the way the media works in tandem with (or sometimes against) police investigations. A string of well-placed clues makes this a suspenseful tale filled with intriguing secrets, and Jean is revealed to be a character of deep complexity.

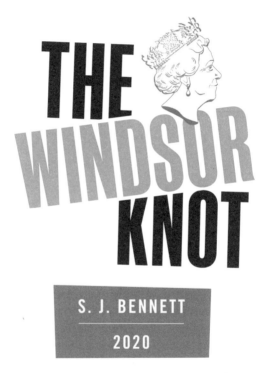

THE WINDSOR KNOT

S. J. BENNETT

2020

DATE READ

Who could resist the enticing premise that Queen Elizabeth II secretly solves crimes alongside carrying out her royal duties? As a shrewd judge of character with the power and access to examine things that go wrong, she is perfectly placed to discreetly take matters into her own hands.

In the first book of this delightful mystery series, the Queen is preparing for her ninetieth birthday celebrations. But when a guest is found dead in a Windsor Castle bedroom and the MI5 investigation goes awry, Her Majesty prudently joins the investigation along with Rozie Oshodi, her assistant private secretary. Filled with wickedly funny banter between royals and political chicanery at the palace, this suspenseful story keeps us guessing as the Queen stays ahead of the game.

Author S. J. Bennett wrote several books for teenagers before starting this wonderfully unique series of adult mysteries. Having once applied for the position as the Queen's private secretary, the author now fictionally lives out this dream job in the clever and resourceful character of Rozie. She and the Queen make a sensational detective team who crack crimes set amidst all the pomp and pageantry of royal circles.

THE TERRACOTTA DOG

ANDREA CAMILLERI * 1996
(TRANSLATED BY STEPHEN SARTARELLI)

Imagine discovering the intertwined skeletons of a man and woman concealed within the hidden grotto of a sealed mountain cave. Who are they? And why are they watched over by a life-size terracotta dog? The intelligent and pragmatic Inspector Montalbano becomes obsessed with solving this fifty-year-old mystery as well as the case of a local robbery. Joined by a diligent team from the police force, his investigation leads him to delve into Sicily's intriguing history and the horrors of the Second World War. Meanwhile, he wrangles with the modern Mafia who intimidate the local community. He must also avoid being distracted by a bevy of beautiful women. This charismatic detective is notable for not only his determined no-nonsense investigations, but also his humour and honourable loyalty. Prepare to be transported to Italy by this highly entertaining brainteaser with a story full of clues and vibrant characters.

Camilleri's much-loved crime fiction led to the long-running *Inspector Montalbano* TV series. This book brings the colours and flavours of Sicily to life while presenting a highly intriguing puzzle that is steeped in folklore and secrets from the past.

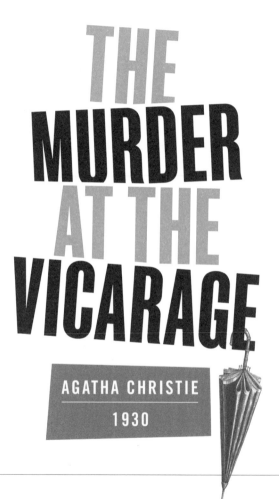

THE MURDER AT THE VICARAGE

AGATHA CHRISTIE

1930

In the quaint village of St Mary Mead, life isn't as peaceful as it first seems. Police are confounded by the sudden murder of Colonel Protheroe, a wealthy and nasty man so disliked that it seems like everyone has a motive. Could it have been Lawrence Redding, a painter who fought in the First World War? Or Anne Protheroe, the Colonel's beautiful second wife? Or Gladys Cram, the young secretary spotted carrying a suitcase into the woods at midnight? Only the shrewdly intelligent Miss Marple can untangle a case this intricate. As plots of conspiracy, burglary, impersonation and adultery are revealed, we discover there is so much more simmering beneath the surface of this sleepy English community.

Christie crafts such a gripping labyrinthine mystery with a wide cast of intriguing characters that there's little chance of us getting ahead of the game. But that's what makes this writer one of the 'Queens of Crime' and the world's most translated author. This is the first full-length novel that introduces us to Miss Marple, who appears as a cunning amateur detective in many more tales. This elderly super-sleuth with a twinkle in her eyes always has time to gossip.

THE BUTCHER'S HOOK

Most novels set in eighteenth-century London about a young woman from a prosperous family characterise her as compliant and well mannered. However, Anne Jaccob, the heroine of this thrilling and unusual story, possesses an intense agency and wilful spirit to get what she wants no matter the cost. Her father has arranged for her to marry Mr Onions, a calculating older man. But Anne is enamoured with Fub, a roguishly handsome and confident young butcher. This romance is ignited by disturbing forces that inspire Anne to take drastic action. The drama of their situation and the secrets revealed about Anne's past make this an increasingly tense read as the story progresses. Filled with rich Dickensian detail, this novel offers a truly atmospheric and hair-raising reading experience.

Janet Ellis is a well-known TV presenter and actress, but she is also a talented writer who has created an evocative period drama. Anne is a truly unforgettable and formidable protagonist. She is savvy enough to see the shortcomings of those around her and play them to her own advantage. Her mesmerising and tantalising story is filled with well-plotted intrigue that keeps us gripped to the final page.

THE MITFORD MURDERS

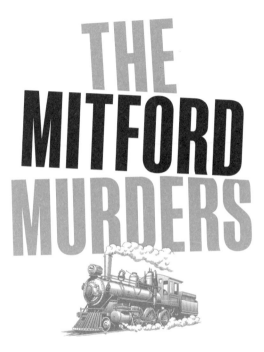

JESSICA FELLOWES * 2017

Prepare to be swept back to the twenties with this tantalising story of impoverished Londoner Louisa Cannon when she attains a coveted position with the Mitford family at their English countryside manor. There she becomes chaperone and confidante to the endearing daughters of the family. Meanwhile, a woman is murdered on a train and police are baffled as to who the perpetrator might be, but railway officer Guy Sullivan is determined to find the truth. Louisa and teenager Nancy Mitford have their own suspicions and search for the killer themselves. Though the events of this novel are fictitious, they are based on the historic unsolved murder case of Florence Nightingale Shore, goddaughter of her famous namesake, and the Mitfords are based on a real aristocratic English family. An evocative blend of fact and fiction are combined in this tale, which starts a series reminiscent of the golden age of detective fiction.

Jessica Fellowes, niece of Julian Fellowes, is well-suited for writing a thrilling mystery having authored the companion books to the famed *Downton Abbey* TV series. This is a tale of high intrigue awash with sumptuous historical detail that evokes the feel of a bygone England.

EARTHLY DELIGHTS

KERRY GREENWOOD * 2004

Corinna Chapman overhauls her life when she divorces her husband and leaves her dull accounting job to open a bakery. Instead of crunching numbers, she spends her time concocting delicious pastries and muffins. By day the bakery is busy with a steady trade in Melbourne's business district, but by night the neighbourhood's seedier side emerges and she's confronted by crime and murder on her doorstep. With her new business and even her cat under threat, Corinna becomes an amateur sleuth and teams up with a hunky private detective. As their investigation progresses, they discover that there are mysteries occurring in her neighbourhood more darkly wondrous than they ever imagined. Filled with intrigue and the aroma of freshly baked bread, this is a novel that truly titillates the senses.

Though Australian author Kerry Greenwood established her talent for historical mysteries with her much-loved Phryne Fisher books, this novel launches the start of a charismatic new female detective. Corinna is independent, clever and sympathetic, and has a whip-smart sense of humour. This is a story filled with colourful characters that we wish we could meet and culinary delights that we wish we could eat.

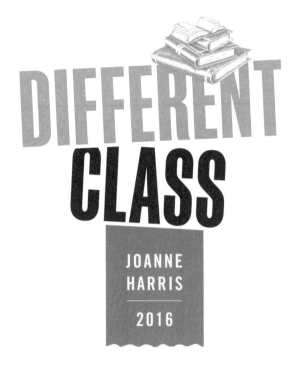

DIFFERENT CLASS

JOANNE
HARRIS

2016

Imagine if a novel were like a gripping and skilful game of chess. The characters in this book are locked in a psychological battle against each other in a story that plays out over twenty-five years. The setting is St Oswald's, a boys' church school steeped in tradition whose reputation has fallen under public scrutiny following a series of scandalous events – including murder. Chapters alternate between the year 1981, when a troubled boy kept a journal about his time at the school, and 2005, when ageing form-master Roy 'Quaz' Straitley recounts substantial changes occurring at the school. This is a dramatic tale of conflicting ideologies, lifelong secrets and the social evolution of an institution built upon conservative values.

Joanne Harris may be best known for her sumptuous novel *Chocolat*, but she also has a talent for crafting a highly original mystery. Unlikeable characters gradually appear in a more sympathetic light once the constraints and insidious ideologies that have shaped them are revealed. The tightly plotted drama of this novel plays out in a way that is exciting and surprising, but it also says something meaningful about our shifting sense of values.

WHY SHOOT A BUTLER?

GEORGETTE HEYER * 1966

The central detective in most murder mysteries is usually charming. But barrister Frank Amberley, the amateur sleuth intent on solving this case, is excessively arrogant and described as 'the rudest man in London'. At the same time he is always one step ahead of the bumbling local police force. Heyer adds wonderful humour to her story by poking fun at her pompous hero while building an intriguing case involving a murdered butler, a mysterious heroine and a country-house party attended by a cast of suspicious characters. Many twists and turns ensue after a dramatic opening, and there is a suspenseful romance. This book seems like it would be the first in a series as it features a group of wickedly memorable characters, but it's a stand-alone mystery which makes for perfect late-night reading.

This novel was first serialised in 1933 as *Suspected!* and is dedicated to the author's husband George Ronald Rougier, who collaborated with her. Although Heyer published a dozen detective novels early in her writing career, she's best known as the author of many bestselling Regency and Georgian historical romances. However, her mysteries are also filled with great wit, cracking dialogue and suspenseful plots.

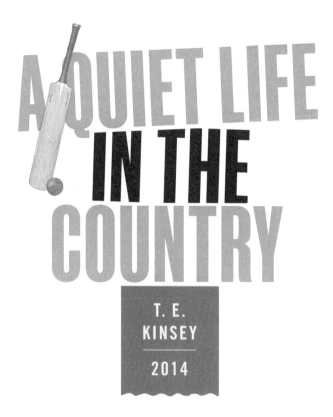

A QUIET LIFE IN THE COUNTRY

T. E.
KINSEY

2014

When Lady Emily Hardcastle moves from London to a large country house with her maid Florence, she hopes for a peaceful existence where she can distance herself from her secret past. But when a body is found in the woods, Emily and Flo can't resist joining in the investigation, as the police seem to be on the wrong track. Though many of the locals are keen to put their best foot forward with this new upper-class lady in their midst, rural rivalries emerge and secrets come to the surface. The cast includes a thief, a group of ragtime musicians, a newly engaged couple, a cricket team and a smattering of aristocratic snobs. It seems like almost everyone might be a suspect, and as Emily and Flo root out the truth, the story of their own intriguingly adventurous past emerges. This lively duo makes for a brilliantly entertaining team of detectives couched in a nostalgic Edwardian setting.

T. E. Kinsey began by self-publishing his stories about the endearing characters of Emily and Florence, which have since sparked a much-loved series of mysteries. They are as much tales of convivial friendship as they are about murder.

ARTISTS IN CRIME

NGAIO MARSH * 1938

It's difficult to conduct a balanced investigation into a murder when you're in love with one of the suspects. That's the dilemma in which Inspector Roderick Alleyn finds himself, having fallen for painter Agatha Troy. A beguiling model is bizarrely murdered with a dagger while she's in the midst of posing at an artists' retreat hosted by Troy. Though Alleyn is determined to root out the killer amongst the group of aristocrats and bohemians who were at the scene, he must consider how Troy herself might have been involved. This adds a simmering tension to this tale, which brings to life interwar England with a cast of fascinatingly suspicious personalities. A string of clues and tense scenes keeps us guessing till the killer's identity is dramatically revealed.

New Zealand author Ngaio Marsh is considered one of the 'Queens of Crime' that emerged out of the golden age of detective fiction. Although this is the sixth novel in her detective books which feature policeman Alleyn, it's one where we learn much more about this sleuth's private life. His conflict between the private and professional is intensely felt, making this a story of great psychological conflict as well as thrilling mystery.

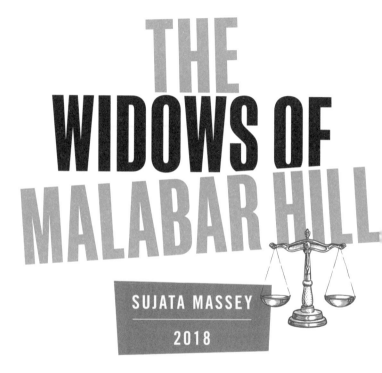

THE WIDOWS OF MALABAR HILL

SUJATA MASSEY

2018

This novel presents an entrancing historical murder mystery with a feminist slant set in 1920s Bombay. Perveen Mistry isn't daunted by being one of the first female lawyers in India. In fact, this makes her all the more determined to prove herself, especially when something about a will left by a wealthy mill owner doesn't make sense. His widows all express a desire to donate their inheritance to a charity, which will leave them penniless. Perveen journeys to visit these women, who practise strict seclusion as part of their religion, to ensure they know their rights. However, she quickly finds herself embroiled in a larger crime as the estate trustee is found murdered. The case not only leads her on a thrilling journey of discovery, but prompts her to reflect on the tragic events of her own life which have led her to determinedly seek justice for women.

As the recipient of several Agatha Awards and having won the Mary Higgins Clark Award for this novel, Sujata Massey has established herself as one of the most exciting and cutting-edge mystery writers working today. Perveen Mistry is not only an endearing and clever character, but also based on two trailblazing female lawyers from India's history.

CAUGHT

LISA MOORE

2013

Young Slaney has just escaped from prison, and with breathtaking suspense we follow his journey as he tries to evade capture and find a new place for himself in the outside world. Parallel to this is the story of Detective Patterson, who hopes to gain a much-needed promotion by bringing the escapee to justice. Their episodic tales lead to encounters with many fascinating characters, including a lonely bride, an eccentric gambler and an ardent reader who drops every book she finishes into the ocean. What's so entrancing about this novel is the way we come to ardently root for both Slaney and Patterson as we read their suspenseful accounts in alternating chapters. But of course, seeing a happy ending for one of them will necessarily cause a devastating conclusion for the other. This story is both tense and beautifully meditative as it builds to a triumphant ending.

Canadian author Lisa Moore began her career as a visual artist and something of this translates to her finely crafted descriptions on the page. Having been incarcerated for four years, Slaney is awed by the sensations of the world with all its vividly evoked scents and dazzling colours. The immediacy of this tale is utterly gripping.

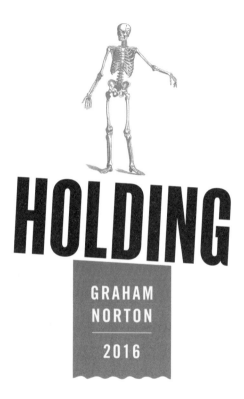

HOLDING

GRAHAM
NORTON

2016

Not much happens in the small Irish village of Duneen, so it's not surprising that the local gossipmongers get busy gabbing when human bones are uncovered at a building site. The area's only policeman, Sergeant P. J. Collins, goes to investigate. He discovers the many layers to this case when certain local secrets that have been buried for twenty-five years are revealed. Norton sympathetically writes about how Collins is a man that struggles with his weight – not only because his elderly housekeeper Mrs Meany cooks him so many hearty meals, but also because eating gives him such emotional comfort. There's also a complicated relationship between three ageing sisters who live in the village's finest house, which is like something out of a Gothic tale. As this compelling mystery unfolds, the characters' tender emotions are movingly revealed, as many are burdened by feelings of isolation and longing.

Graham Norton is such a beloved comedian and TV presenter that it's a pleasure to discover he's also a talented writer whose strongly plotted tale is filled with intriguing secrets and delightfully quirky characters. It's the kind of gripping mystery to keep reading deep into the night.

UNRAVELLING OLIVER

LIZ NUGENT * 2013

Oliver is a man born into difficult circumstances who achieves great success by cunningly hiding his origins, but what happens when he must confront the truth of his past? This clever novel gradually reveals this enigmatic and selfish man's history while telling a suspenseful story concerning his wife Alice and their circle of friends. A number of unconventional relationships are presented with colourfully distinct personalities, including a regal French lady, an egotistical actress and a repressed gay man. By following these characters' points of view, we gradually piece together the mystery of Oliver's true identity. There is a lightness of touch to this tale, with many endearingly human and humorous moments which work alongside the story's central crime.

Before becoming an award-winning Irish author, Liz Nugent had a career in the theatre, which clearly shows in her flair for writing dramatic novels with captivating characters. This story is also skilfully arranged to slowly reveal information through the limited perspective of the characters relating different pieces of the puzzle. They don't always appreciate the gravity of the information they individually hold, which makes reading this story a particularly nail-biting and absorbing experience.

JACK OF SPADES

JOYCE CAROL OATES

2015

The fictional anti-hero of this dramatic mystery is Andrew J. Rush who is a highly respected author that has been dubbed by the press to be the 'gentleman's Stephen King'. Longing to escape the confines of his literary reputation, he writes a series of lurid thrillers using the pseudonym 'Jack of Spades'. But when his authorial identity runs the risk of being revealed and a woman named C. W. Haider accuses him of plagiarism, his life becomes unstable and prone to the same kind of violence found in his sensational novels. There are secrets lurking in basements and mysterious activities in the middle of the night. In following a string of clues, Rush discovers that it's not so easy to neatly divide his identity. This fast-paced, electrifying read follows a writer's descent into madness.

While this is a great tale of psychological suspense, it's also a playful commentary on the writing life, as Joyce Carol Oates is herself a well-respected author who has written a number of thrillers using a pseudonym. Oates has a riveting way of exploring the disaster and derangement that can ensue if darker subterranean aspects of consciousness are allowed free rein.

THE THURSDAY MURDER CLUB

RICHARD OSMAN * 2020

When four septuagenarian residents of a retirement community formed a club to look over the cases of unsolved mysteries, they never expected a murder case would appear in their own back yard. This charismatic group plunge into vigorously investigating this new crime. Between them they have a wealth of experience, knowledge and connections – especially high-spirited former spy Elizabeth. What's so compelling about this novel is that on top of the mystery surrounding the murders which occur in the story, we are led to wonder about the enigma of these characters' pasts. Many of the younger people around them, including police officers and characters from the local community, overlook and dismiss them. This engrossing tale shows that there is much more to these spirited retirees than meets the eye.

Famed quiz-show host Richard Osman has quickly established himself as a major mystery novelist with this chart-topping debut novel and its fast-selling follow-up. Widely described as a publishing phenomenon, this author has a talent for writing truly beguiling tales. This story is rich in detail and poignantly describes the dilemmas of individuals who are normally considered over the hill.

THE NO.1 LADIES' DETECTIVE AGENCY

ALEXANDER MCCALL SMITH * 1998

After receiving an inheritance from her father, Mma Precious Ramotswe moves to Botswana's capital to buy a house, a van and an office space to launch the country's first female private detective agency. She's independent, empathetic and unafraid to use a gun when it's needed. We follow the practicalities of starting a business as well as her first cases involving a missing husband, a doctor that might be an imposter and tracking down a boy who has been abducted. Her experiences are as much about getting to know the idiosyncratic members of her community and the country's beautiful landscape as it is about solving crimes. Though she confronts instances of cruelty and selfishness, Precious is warm-hearted, humorous and always seeks joy in life.

This novel was first published in 1998 and launched a series which has included new instalments almost every year for over two decades. Though it had only a small readership at first, the series has gone on to produce international bestsellers and a successful TV series. Many of the other books in the series feature more concentrated mysteries, but this is where we're first introduced to one of the most vibrantly original sleuths in all of detective fiction.

MURDER AT THE MANSIONS

SARA ROSETT * 2022

Despite being born into the aristocracy, Olive Belgrave must support herself and has worked hard to become established as the preeminent discreet sleuth for the high-society set of 1920s London. In this story, Olive has just moved into a mansion block that includes maid service and a group of intriguing neighbours. When one of her latest local friends confesses that she saw a dead body which has since disappeared, Olive and her charismatic buddy Jasper investigate whether there is something more sinister going on in this posh building. Through a series of amusing encounters with her idiosyncratic neighbours, she uncovers rivalries, affairs and suspicious activity aplenty. This is a story filled with sparkling banter, mistaken identities, atmospheric descriptions of English high society and puzzling mysteries.

This is the seventh novel in Rosett's successful High Society Lady Detective series and at this point of the series, Olive has developed into a well-rounded, cunning sleuth. This book was inspired by Agatha Christie, which really shows in the author's ability to plant several red herrings and keep us guessing till the dramatic end. There's a charming light-hearted tone to the series and this mystery is Olive's best yet!

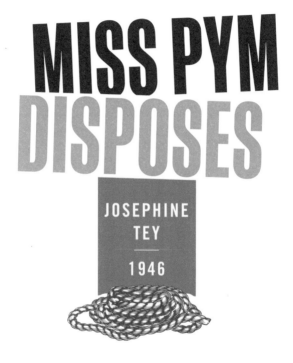

MISS PYM DISPOSES

JOSEPHINE TEY

1946

An inheritance allows Lucy Pym the ability to indulge in pursuing her favourite subject: psychology. She writes an extremely popular book about it and gets invited to guest lecture at a physical training college. There she becomes close to an array of bright students. Though the girls' training focuses on building healthy bodies and many seem destined for success, Miss Pym begins to wonder if such rigorous exercise is good for their mental health. Her concern comes to the fore when a horrible incident in the gymnasium makes her see that some of these girls might not be as good-natured as they first appear. Using her psychological expertise she endeavours to deduce whether the tragedy was an accident or something more sinister.

Josephine Tey wrote a separate series of books with the hero Inspector Alan Grant and this 1946 novel isn't a conventional detective tale. However, it's a unique stand-alone mystery which raises absorbing questions about intentions, motives and what should be considered a crime. Be aware that this book contains some dated references. However, it's a thought-provoking portrait of a society in a state of flux from the point of view of an unforgettably clever heroine.

A MEDITATION ON MURDER

ROBERT THOROGOOD * 2015

The Caribbean island of Saint Marie seems like paradise, and Aslan Kennedy's retreat for wealthy holidaymakers appears to be the picture of tranquillity, but when Aslan is murdered, we discover things aren't so idyllic on these tropical shores. British Detective Inspector Richard Poole is sent to investigate what at first appears to be an open and shut case. There were only five other people inside the locked room where Aslan was killed and one has already confessed to the murder, but Poole knows that there's more to this curious case. Along with his endearing sidekick Camille, he's determined to solve this crime and get off the swelteringly hot island. Though the gorgeous setting is described in tempting detail, Poole is a complete stick-in-the-mud who refuses to change out of his dark woollen suit and join in the relaxed attitude of the community. This makes for an ongoing source of comedy paired with a classic whodunnit plot that keeps us guessing.

Robert Thorogood created his idiosyncratic character of a 'Copper in the Caribbean' for the hit *Death in Paradise* BBC crime-drama series before writing him into a series of murder mystery novels. This case is where it all began.

CAN YOU HEAR ME?

ELENA VARVELLO
(TRANSLATED BY ALEX VALENTE)

2016

Elia spends his days swimming in a local pond and developing a nervous crush on his friend's mother. Though the story begins feeling like an ordinary tale about a teenage boy on his school holiday during the hot summer of 1978, things quickly turn sinister. Tensions in this small Italian town are rising due to unemployment and news of a local boy going missing. Elia's father Ettore begins acting suspiciously and disappears for lengthy periods of time. The narrative alternates between Elia's memories of this fated sweat-soaked summer and a girl's account of being picked up by Ettore, who drives her to a remote location. What unfolds is a mystery filled with riveting tension and a captivating coming-of-age tale steeped in nostalgia.

Lauded Italian author Elena Varvello is also a poet, and the elegance of her prose enhances this inventive and bewitching psychological thriller. While Elia struggles with the normal issues of a growing boy, he's also burdened with his parents' increasing despondency. The novel develops a progressive emotional poignancy at the same time as its unsettling atmosphere increases.

THE CLOCK STRIKES TWELVE

PATRICIA WENTWORTH * 1944

The Paradine family's New Year celebrations are abruptly halted when grumpy-but-loveable old patriarch James is found murdered. Police are flummoxed – everyone at the country estate has either an alibi or a story which keeps changing. Of course, just because many members of this bickering clan are unlikeable and money-grubbing doesn't mean that they're guilty. Luckily, Miss Maud Silver is on the case. Nothing gets past this clever, retired English governess who enjoys quoting the poetry of Tennyson. She works closely with Scotland Yard and with her mild manners has the ability to lull those she interrogates into revealing more than they intend. This supremely plotted tale is full of compelling family secrets and servants who are always watching.

Prolific early-twentieth-century British author Patricia Wentworth wrote thirty-two whodunnit novels featuring this genial super-sleuth. Often compared with Miss Marple due to her advanced age and seemingly harmless appearance, Miss Silver has unique charms which make her an exceptional and singular private eye. In this novel she really comes into her own. Wentworth also created a few other detective series as well as a plethora of stand-alone mysteries.

THE BODIES IN THE LIBRARY

MARTY WINGATE

2019

Every Agatha Christie fan dreams of what it would be like to work alongside a detective to uncover a murder, but no one ever imagines they would end up as the body. Except that's what happens when a fan-fiction writers' group meets at a Georgian home in Bath, which contains an extensive and impressive first-edition library including many volumes of golden-age mystery stories, and one of the participants ends up dead. Their meeting had been organised by the library's new curator Hayley Burke, who has secretly never read a mystery in her life. But when local police are baffled by the case, she steps in to investigate it, save her job and learn the skills it takes to solve a whodunnit. The clever concept of this novel is carried out with cheeky good humour as Hayley sifts through clues, gets assistance from the library owner's cat and investigates a range of equally untrustworthy suspects.

Having written two other series of cosy murder mysteries, Marty Wingate launched the First Edition Library Mystery series with this novel about a hilariously unlikely detective. Bibliophiles will swoon at the story's lavish descriptions of a beautiful library of rare books.

MAISIE DOBBS

JACQUELINE WINSPEAR * 2003

Some people seem to have been born to become detectives. In this novel we're introduced to Maisie Dobbs who possesses the innate intelligence, plucky spirit and ingenuity for the job. Though she's born as a poor girl in pre-war England and begins work as a maid in an aristocratic house during her adolescence, her kindly employer recognises her unique capacity for learning and becomes her patroness. When the country goes to war, Maisie enlists to work as a nurse overseas. After surviving the heartbreak and horrors of this turbulent time, she embarks on her private-eye business determined not only to bring criminals to justice, but also to heal those suffering from the after-effects of the First World War. In her first mystery, Maisie investigates what appears to be a simple case about a woman suspected of being unfaithful to her husband, but it leads her on a path that includes solving a murder and discovering the truth about what occurred during the war.

Winspear has steadily produced over a dozen novels starring this empathetic heroine. They are a unique blend of historical fiction and psychologically rich mystery that emotionally reckons with the long-term effects of national conflict.

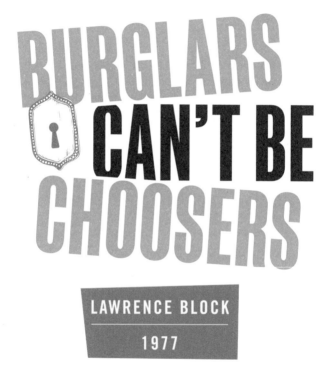

BURGLARS CAN'T BE CHOOSERS

LAWRENCE BLOCK

1977

A gentleman burglar is an unlikely hero. Though Bernie Rhodenbarr is a thief and an expert at picking locks, he maintains certain principles: to only steal from the rich and never commit acts of physical violence. This charming upper-class criminal's schemes are well planned and carefully executed – until one job goes very badly wrong. Bernie is commissioned to steal a small blue box from a New York City apartment, but during the heist he's intercepted by two policemen who also discover a body on the premises. Before they can arrest him, he escapes, but now he's the prime suspect and must track down the real murderer before he is captured. A fast-paced mystery ensues, which involves almost every character in its tangle of intrigue. This wickedly funny story introduces a loveable rogue who has subsequently appeared in a dozen novels featuring his misadventures.

Crime writer Lawrence Block is also famous for the Matthew Scudder series which features a recovering alcoholic PI, but the Rhodenbarr books are much lighter and playful in tone. In subsequent stories, Bernie acquires a cat and a secondhand bookstore in Greenwich Village, which he partially funds through his criminal activities.

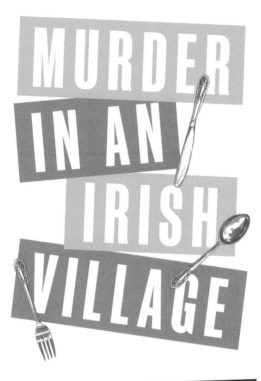

MURDER IN AN IRISH VILLAGE

CARLENE O'CONNOR * 2016

The small village of Kilbane may seem like a picture postcard of rural Irish life, but it's also full of local intrigue and, in the case of this story, a terrible murder. The O'Sullivan clan run a local bistro which the eldest daughter Siobhan has taken charge of since the death of her parents in a tragic accident. One day the brother of the man imprisoned for their deaths comes around to make trouble. When this suited man is found stabbed in the family bistro, the guards suspect Siobhan's eldest brother James is the culprit. To be sure, the villagers get busy gossiping about the case, and feisty Siobhan is determined to prove her brother's innocence. A series of compelling discoveries and nail-biting confrontations lead her to uncover the truth about this case. Along the way we get to intimately know this independent red-head as she cleverly uncovers clues and develops a romantic relationship with a macho cop investigating the crime.

This book launched a mystery series involving the O'Sullivan siblings. The charming location is brought to life with evocative Irish dialect and a series of endearing characters who are also suspects.

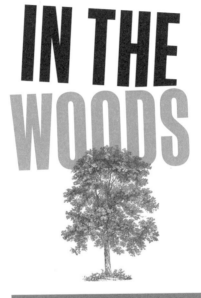

IN THE WOODS

TANA FRENCH * 2007

DATE READ

What if a deeply traumatic event from the distant past were the key to uncovering a present-day mystery? Detective Rob Ryan is charged with investigating a case which feels eerily familiar to him: a girl is found murdered in the same woods where his friends vanished when he was a boy. He was the only survivor of this horrific event but can't recall any specific details about what happened. Now he must plunder his locked memories while searching for clues to solve this new crime. Soon his professional reputation and sanity are on the line. Alongside his friend and partner Detective Cassie Maddox, he encounters red herrings, police bureaucracy and tantalising secrets in this suspense-filled tale. French excels at writing fully rounded characters and describing the dark corners of human nature while crafting a story which is difficult to put down.

This exceptional book won numerous mystery and crime awards. It's the first case in the fictional Dublin Murder Squad series, which presents a number of stand-alone cases focusing on different detectives. The first and second books in this series were also turned into an eight-episode drama by the BBC and RTÉ.

MURDER ON CAPE COD

MADDIE DAY

2018

The tourist town of Westham on Cape Cod seems like a sleepy and idyllic location, but sinister things are occurring in the shadows. One foggy night, Mackenzie 'Mac' Almeida is on her way home from a Cozy Capers book club meeting when she discovers a body. Not only is the victim a handyman with whom she recently had a public argument, but also he's been stabbed with a very distinctive fishing knife owned by her brother Derrick. Naturally, Mac is eager to prove her and her family's innocence. Detective Haskins warns her to leave it to the professionals, but Mac's book club are eager to help investigate, as each member has unique crime-solving capabilities. This story is filled with an utterly charming group of characters – including a charismatic African grey parrot. Alongside an intriguing story filled with potential suspects, there's a sweet romance which plays out between Mac and an adorable chef named Tim.

Maddie Day has a passion for cooking herself which is infused in her story-telling. This is the first book in her Cozy Capers Book Group Mysteries series where amateur sleuths get the chance to investigate real crimes in a wonderfully atmospheric setting.

GOODNIGHT BEAUTIFUL

AIMEE
MOLLOY

2020

When Sam and Annie get married, they move to his rural hometown in the hope of settling into a quiet life, only to find themselves plunged into a gripping mystery. Sam establishes his business as a psychological therapist in a posh new office, but he doesn't realise his sessions can be overheard through a vent in the room above it. At first listening in on his juicy conversations where women from the local community divulge the most intimate details about their lives is just a bad habit for Annie. But when an amorous French client enters his therapy room, things become more unsettling. And when Sam doesn't return home from work on Valentine's Day, Annie becomes frantic with worry. Who can she trust? Not only is there the emotional question over whether this couple's relationship will survive, but also there's the tense possibility that they might not even live through this puzzling ordeal. This is a real edge-of-the-seat thriller with plenty of plot twists and a beguiling unreliable narrator.

Aimee Molloy is a bestselling author of fiction and non-fiction. It's refreshing to read a mystery where the man goes missing instead of the woman, and there are many more innovative aspects of this engrossing tale.

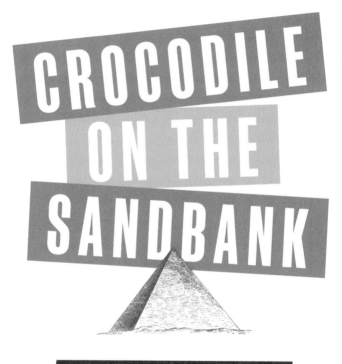

CROCODILE ON THE SANDBANK

ELIZABETH PETERS * 1975

This light-hearted historical mystery stars an unconventional Victorian woman who embarks on an atmospheric adventure through Egypt. When feisty feminist Amelia Peabody inherits a fortune from her scholarly father, she can finally indulge in her passion for exploring remnants from the past while journeying up the Nile. Though Amelia and her companion Evelyn are far more interested in finding artefacts than romance, their lives become intimately entangled with two brothers who are uncovering curious wonders buried under a former pharaoh's capital city. Amelia scoffs at local supernatural tales, but the group have tricky encounters with a mummy that roams through the desert at night. However, the true drama of this story is embedded in the Egyptian landscape and historical facts which bring it so vividly to life.

This is the first book which features Amelia Peabody, the determined, intelligent heroine of the author's long-running popular series that includes twenty volumes. Elizabeth Peters was the pen name of Barbara Mertz who wrote other series of novels using different pseudonyms. Prior to these mystery novels, she published two highly respected non-fiction books on ancient Egypt which clearly informed her fiction.

CASE
HISTORIES

KATE
ATKINSON

2004

Atkinson's novel begins with three separate cases that private investigator Jackson Brodie has been charged with solving. They involve girls who have been missing for many years and a murdered girl whose killer was never identified. People involved in each of these crimes describe their subjective understanding of what occurred. The story then launches into Brodie's perspective as he makes inquiries and discoveries which link these seemingly unrelated incidents. As we get further details about these mysterious cases, we also learn more about Brodie's own complicated and fascinating past working in the army and the police force before launching his own detective enterprise. The author excels at showing how the truth can only be arrived at by considering different points of view. It's also splendid how the university city of Cambridge is brought to life in a series of noteworthy scenes.

Kate Atkinson is an award-winning author of several works of literary fiction as well as the Jackson Brodie detective novels. The first three books in this series have been turned into a three-part BBC TV adaptation. Though these books don't shy from exposing the ugliness of the world, they also show how the past can be reckoned with in order to achieve happiness.

AN EXPERT IN MURDER

NICOLA UPSON * 2008

Who could make a better super-sleuth than a famous author of mysteries? In this first novel of Nicola Upson's inventive historical mystery series, we're introduced to a fictionalised version of crime writer and playwright Josephine Tey, who appears here as both the heroine and the detective. Set in 1930s London, this novel describes Tey's journey to attend her own debut stage play of *Richard of Bordeaux* and how she becomes involved in a perplexing murder case. Tey teams up with Detective Inspector Archie Penrose to investigate the flamboyant and suspicious theatre troupe, as the investigators are certain one of the performers or crew is behind the crime. The colourful lives in this interwar environment are wonderfully evoked. It's also a case as layered as any from the golden age of detective fiction but features more modern, in-depth psychological portraits.

Upson's novels are both a loving tribute to Josephine Tey and a clever crime series in their own right. The author initially wanted to write a biography of Tey, but there are so few historical records about her life that Upson chose instead to create these atmospheric and entertaining fictional tales about Tey's life.

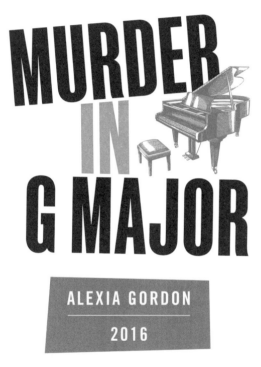

MURDER IN G MAJOR

ALEXIA GORDON

2016

African-American classical musician Gethsemane Brown moves to Ireland to start a new life for herself, as she's acquired a teaching position at a rural school. Though it's a challenge trying to form these unruly boys into an orchestra, she's driven by a passion for music and is determined to keep her good humour. The landscape of the countryside is vividly evoked as she takes residence of a gorgeous cliff-side cottage. But she soon finds that she has an unlikely housemate in the form of a restless ghost. This distempered individual is composer Eamon McCarthy. Many years ago, his and his wife Orla's deaths were ruled to be a murder-suicide. Now he is determined to have his name cleared. He entreats reluctant Gethsemane to help investigate this mystery, but she unexpectedly becomes a new target for the killer.

Alexia Gordon's playful series of supernatural mysteries give a refreshing take on some well-trodden tropes. Gethsemane is an unlikely detective, but she's so personable and clever that she's more than able to uncover what secrets are lurking in the Irish countryside. These novels are also infused with a wonderful love of music, which adds a distinct tone to the atmosphere.

THE RETURN OF SHERLOCK HOLMES

ARTHUR CONAN DOYLE * 1905

What happens when the world's most famous detective is killed off by his own creator? There is public outcry! Doyle wrote of Sherlock Holmes's dramatic 'death' in his 1893 short story 'The Final Problem', but the author received many disgruntled letters from his fans, and publishers offered him increasingly large sums of money to bring Holmes back. Though Doyle was a prolific author in many genres and wanted to focus more on writing historical novels, he finally acquiesced to demand in the years 1903–1904 by producing a compelling series of new Sherlock Holmes detective tales for magazines. They were subsequently published as this collection in which it's explained how Holmes survived his final battle with Moriarty and returned to London after a stint of hiding in the Far East.

These beguiling stories show Holmes at the height of his powers of deduction tracking down a missing duke's son, deciphering the meaning of a series of cryptic stick figures, untangling a blackmail scam and solving many more perplexing murders. And Holmes's return reminds us of the camaraderie and friendship he shares with Dr Watson, which has become even stronger after their time apart.

THE VANISHED BRIDE

BELLA
ELLIS

2019

There's an irresistible charm to imagining that the legendary Brontë sisters might have been amateur sleuths before they became novelists. The year is 1845 and in a small Yorkshire town, a wife and mother named Elizabeth Chester goes missing. All that's left is a pool of blood in her room and two young children. A nearby parson's daughters are horrified but intrigued by this mysterious case and decide to investigate it themselves as 'lady detectives'. Charlotte, Emily and Anne set out from Haworth determined to discover the truth. Along the way, they encounter plenty of resistance, as they're perceived as women who aren't keeping their proper place. However, the dogged trio won't be dissuaded. Each sister's distinctive personality is brilliantly observed in the novel's witty dialogue. What they uncover is a story of menace, intrigue and deception all set in this atmospheric northern-England setting.

Successful author Rowan Coleman created the Brontë-esque pseudonym of Bella Ellis to launch this series of mystery novels. Like many, Coleman was beguiled by the sisters' lives when she first visited the Brontë Parsonage Museum when she was a girl. This first novel is both a loving tribute to the great Victorian authors and a truly spooky crime story.

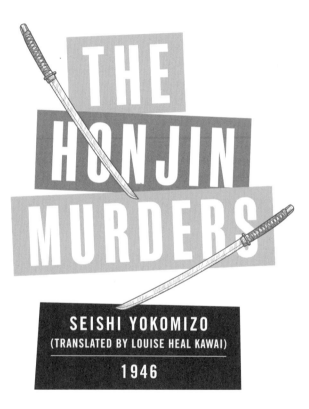

THE HONJIN MURDERS

SEISHI YOKOMIZO
(TRANSLATED BY LOUISE HEAL KAWAI)

1946

On a wintry evening in 1937, the prestigious Ichiyanagi family gather to celebrate the marriage of their eldest son. But on the wedding night, the household is woken by a terrifying scream and the sound of eerie music. When the clan get up to investigate, they discover the newlyweds dead and a blood-soaked samurai sword thrust into the ground with no footprints to be found in the snow surrounding it. No one could have entered or left this isolated mansion so the crime must have been committed by someone in the family or one of their guests. Amateur private detective Kosuke Kindaichi is summoned to investigate. As the case unfolds, we discover details about the history, culture and aesthetics of Japan which are not only fascinating, but prove to be the key to understanding the motive behind these horrendous murders.

Though this novel was first published in Japan in 1946, the first English translation only came out in 2019. It's the first book which features detective Kindaichi who goes on to appear in a further seventy-seven mysteries by this author. Seishi Yokomizo combined his passion for Western detective novels with a knowledge of Japanese society to create a new form of the classic locked-room mystery.

POISON FOR TEACHER

NANCY SPAIN * 1951

A series of bizarre pranks occur at girls' school Radcliff Hall and the headmistress is frantic with worry. Not only are these antics increasingly menacing, but they are also becoming deadly. In desperation, she visits a Baker Street detective agency run by the daring and clever Miriam Birdseye. This ex-revue star joins her friend Natasha to go undercover as teachers at the school to investigate what's really happening. There they encounter a cast of peculiar staff members and disaffected schoolgirls. The plot is thick with blackmail, scandal and sexual affairs, but it's all extremely tongue in cheek. Though there is plenty of intrigue, the entertaining story is primarily concerned with its characters' journeys and witty interactions. For those who like their mysteries infused with humour and absurdity, this outrageous romp will tickle.

Though the author's writing was progressive at the time for its sly subversion of the sexual mores in post-Second-World-War English society, be aware that its satire also contains dated and problematic references to race. In addition to writing a series of detective novels, Nancy Spain was herself a figure of intrigue and scandal who worked as a journalist until her tragic death in a 1964 plane crash.

FINGERSMITH

SARAH WATERS

2002

Steeped in the bawdy atmosphere of Victorian London and the Gothic mystery of a secluded country house, this book revolutionised the historical crime novel. Sue Trinder is an orphan and petty thief tasked with posing as a lady's maid to Maud Lilly who was raised to keep her imposing uncle's stately home and act as his secretary. The narrative alternates between their perspectives and includes many gasp-worthy twists and turns. When the two young women form a romantic connection, they hatch a plan to escape their circumstances and be together. But with so many buried secrets, criminal plans and scheming characters, this resourceful pair don't know if they can really trust anyone – even each other.

Waters summons all the grit and glamour of mid-nineteenth-century England to create a wonderfully evocative and masterfully paced tale. It's a relentlessly intriguing puzzle box filled with the heart-racing passion of romance and a plot so captivating that it's worthy of a late-night reading binge. The novel was nominated for multiple prestigious awards, and Sarah Waters has published several other acclaimed historical novels.

THE HOURS BEFORE DAWN

CELIA FREMLIN * 1958

Louise Henderson is an over-burdened mother struggling to cope with multiple demanding offspring, a baby who cries through the night and a husband unwilling to participate in housework or care for the children. To ease the family's financial worries, they take in an affable woman named Vera Brandon as a lodger. But as Louise feels the frazzling effects of sleep deprivation, she worries that Miss Brandon is overly familiar and has sinister motives for inhabiting their house. Is she spying on Louise and making a play for her husband? There's a judicious balance of funny observations and terrifying moments in this concisely written tale. The story is set in 1950s London when gender demarcation ruled and mental health wasn't a consideration. It's a book which is different from a traditional crime story, as it is more of a psychological suspense in a domestic setting. However, it contains a mystery with many chilling moments as we sympathetically follow Louise's crumbling home life.

This debut won the 1960 Edgar Award for best mystery novel and is viewed as a precursor of the domestic noir. Celia Fremlin also produced over a dozen more novels in a similar vein before her death in 2009.

THE FAMILY CHAO

LAN SAMANTHA CHANG * 2022

The Fine Chao restaurant in Wisconsin has been a fixture of the community for multiple decades and the proprietors' three sons have promising futures, as they've all won scholarships to prestigious colleges. But all that changes when arguments with the family's domineering patriarch Big Leo Chao reach a crisis point and he's found dead after a lavish Christmas celebration. Vicious gossip swirls around the family and the eldest son Dagou is put on trial for his father's murder. His two very different younger brothers scramble to come to terms with their family's turbulent history and uncover what really happened that fateful night. With elements that include a dead stranger's travel bag filled with cash, an illegitimate child's well-kept secrets, a missing dog and a father locked in the freezer, this is a mystery that grows increasingly thrilling as it unfolds. It's a unique and meaningful tale which grapples with issues of racism, corruption and greed. At the same time it is darkly funny, poignant and utterly gripping.

Lan Samantha Chang has won numerous awards and honours for her writing. With this novel, she reimagines Dostoevsky's classic *The Brothers Karamazov* while creating a unique modern-day Chinese-American family mystery.

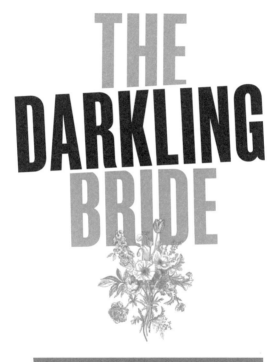

THE DARKLING BRIDE

LAURA ANDERSEN * 2018

Recent college graduate Carragh Ryan takes what at first appears to be a dream job cataloguing a grand library housed at Deeprath Castle in Ireland. She's charged with archiving the old books and ascertaining whether they have any value before they are handed over to the National Trust. However, she finds herself at the centre of a bewitching and dangerous mystery. The Gallagher family have resided at this noble old estate for centuries and terrible deaths have beset members of the clan over multiple generations. Were these a series of unconnected tragedies? Local legend claims that the castle is haunted by a vengeful female spirit. A local investigator is making fresh inquiries into these cold cases and Carragh finds herself drawn into the scandals of this ancient family home. In the quest to discover what really happened, everyone appears to be a suspect and Carragh begins to fear for her life.

This is a sumptuous stand-alone Gothic mystery with a large cast of intriguing characters that moves between multiple timelines. It's filled with family secrets, ghostly presences and an atmospheric setting. Laura Andersen has also written historical trilogies about Anne Boleyn and the Tudors.

THE DECAGON HOUSE MURDERS

YUKITO AYATSUJI * 1987
(TRANSLATED BY HO-LING WONG)

For a group of university students who are part of a mystery club, the opportunity to investigate the murder of a couple on a deserted island off the coast of Japan proves to be too tempting. However, after travelling there, things quickly turn sinister as the club members start being killed off one by one. Kawaminami is a man on the mainland who also has a keen interest in detective stories, and while macabre events unfold on the island, he receives a letter accusing him of murder. He desperately seeks to uncover how this is connected to the island deaths. Meanwhile, club member Ellery races against time to discover the killer and bring the grisly murder of these students to an end. Many thrilling plot twists and shocking disclosures ensue.

Not only did Agatha Christie's *And Then There Were None* influence the plot of Ayatsuji's novel, but it's directly referenced by several characters throughout the book. Ayatsuji has his own unique take on this classic tale and, as with all locked-room mysteries, there are a series of clues in this book which could potentially allow us to solve the case before it's revealed in the story.

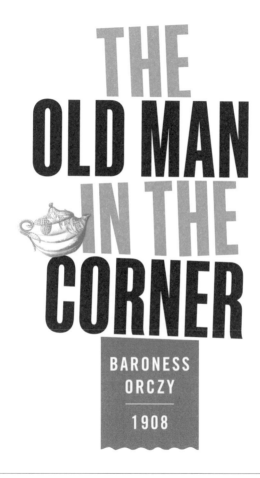

THE OLD MAN IN THE CORNER

BARONESS ORCZY

1908

What if one of the world's most clever detectives could solve crimes without even getting up from his chair? A journalist named Polly Burton converses with a nameless old man while they sit in the corner of a London tea-room. The gentleman happens to believe that if the proper intelligence is applied when considering the known facts, there is no such thing as a mystery in connection with any crime. Polly tests his assertion by presenting him with many sensational cases which have baffled the police. These range from tales of missing spouses to families trying to swindle each other, blackmail schemes and several murders. The eccentric old man solves them using nothing but his powers of deduction while tying complicated knots in a piece of string. Though none of the perpetrators are ever brought to justice, this clever collection shows that tales of mystery are the ultimate brain-teasers!

Though Baroness Orczy was best known for her series of novels featuring the Scarlet Pimpernel, she also regularly wrote detective stories to sell to magazines. In early-twentieth-century England, there was a craze for such tales in the style of *Sherlock Holmes*. Orczy created her own unique and thoroughly entertaining gentleman detective.

BRUNO, CHIEF OF POLICE

MARTIN WALKER * 2008

Having left his traumatic life in the army, Benoît Courrèges or Bruno (as he is affectionally named by the locals) works as a policeman in the sleepy French village of St Denis. Here he spends his time enjoying food, wine, women and working the land surrounding his restored cottage. Everyone knows everyone in this peaceful village. But this idyllic life is shaken by the murder of an elderly Algerian immigrant who appears to have been the victim of a far-right hate crime. Bruno teams up with a young female police officer from Paris to investigate the sordid and complicated political motives behind this case. It leads them to uncover little-known details from French history and the Second World War. What's so charming about this tale is the way Bruno gains the respect of everyone in his community because of his earnest commitment to justice – even when that conflicts with the law of the land.

Over a dozen mysteries in the popular *Bruno, Chief of Police* series have been published since this first volume. Martin Walker is an English journalist who (unsurprisingly) has a holiday home in a southern French village very similar to the one in the novel.

ANDEAN EXPRESS

JUAN DE RECACOECHEA
(TRANSLATED BY ADRIAN ALTHOFF)

2000

Many mystery writers have been inspired by Agatha Christie and in this novel her classic tale *Murder on the Orient Express* is transposed to South America. Ricardo is a high-school graduate making an overnight train journey from Bolivia to Chile in 1952. He's seeking a vacation filled with adventure and romance, but he finds it sooner than he thinks as he becomes enamoured with an eighteen-year-old bride on the train. When her much-despised German husband is found dead, Ricardo knows the culprit must be aboard. The murdered businessman had many enemies and there are a plethora of suspicious individuals including a Franciscan priest, an inebriated Irishman, an affable madam, the bride's mother and a card sharp. Pivotal decisions are made over a poker game. The journey through the atmospheric landscape of the high Andes mountains is vividly described. Recacoechea balances a portrait of the insular nature of upper-class Bolivian society with a villainous story of intrigue.

Juan de Recacoechea was a journalist who lived abroad for long periods of time. His international sensibility is evident in the way he depicts the diverse crowd that populate this locked-room mystery.

RIVERS OF LONDON

BEN AARONOVITCH * 2011

Crime and magic combine in this urban fantasy which follows Peter Grant, a young officer in London's Metropolitan Police. He dreams of becoming a detective and gains a distinct career advantage when a ghost conveys inside information to him about a murder. Peter's paranormal skills are noticed by Detective Chief Inspector Thomas Nightingale who recruits him into a special branch of the Met concerned with the supernatural. Soon after Peter is made an apprentice wizard, he's tasked with two uncanny cases involving bodily possession and two warring gods of the River Thames. Though he learns how to hone his magical ability, he also uses science and logic to solve the mysteries and confront his foes. The narrative voice is laced with humour and wit which ingeniously makes the outlandish occurrences feel relatable. While the story is set in richly depicted twenty-first-century London, it draws upon the historical and mythological background of the capital and the Thames Valley.

Ben Aaronovitch has also written *Doctor Who* serials and spin-off novels. Working on the great stalwart of British fantasy well prepared him for creating his own highly original set of police procedural novels.

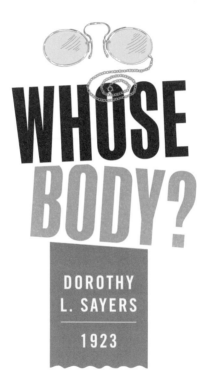

WHOSE BODY?

DOROTHY L. SAYERS

1923

A man enters the bathroom of his London flat one morning to discover a corpse wearing nothing but a pair of golden pince-nez in his tub. Having no clue about the deceased's identity, this gentleman and the police puzzle over who this man was and how he got there. Inspector Sugg suggests that the body must belong to famous financier Sir Reuben Levy who went missing the previous night. However, Inspector Charles Parker, who is investigating Levy's disappearance, sees that the corpse only superficially resembles Levy. Solving this perplexing mystery is just the challenge that Lord Peter Wimsey has been looking for! He's a nobleman who has taken up criminal investigation as a hobby. He has quite the talent for sniffing out the truth, but Wimsey also finds himself in peril as he draws closer to discovering the identity of the murderer. The plot contains a balance of intrigue, tension and humour while the story also wonderfully evokes 1920s London. This first case involving Wimsey introduces him as a charming, funny and loveable gentleman detective.

Though early-twentieth-century author Dorothy L. Sayers started as a poet, she became most popular for her detective fiction. She featured Lord Peter Wimsey in eleven novels.

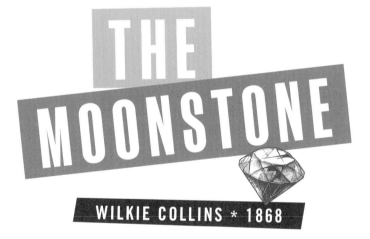

THE
MOONSTONE

WILKIE COLLINS * 1868

At the centre of this classic mystery is a rare diamond which is rumoured to be cursed. It is bequeathed to Rachel Verinder who wears it to a lavish party celebrating her eighteenth birthday at her mother's estate. However, when the diamond disappears, an investigation takes place during which the plethora of suspects include party guests, family members, Rachel's suitors, servants, three Indian jugglers and even Rachel herself. Though renowned detective Sergeant Cuff makes many inquiries and settles upon a certain theory concerning the case, at first nothing can be officially proved. The story is told through letters from people connected with the incident, and by following their subjective accounts, we discover some startling revelations and piece together the truth behind this highly intriguing mystery. Each narrator is wonderfully idiosyncratic and engaging in their own way.

First serialised in Charles Dickens's magazine, *All the Year Round*, this riveting tale is considered a foundational text of the modern detective novel, as it introduced elements which have become mystery-story staples, including an English-country-house setting, a series of false suspects, red herrings, a celebrated investigator and a final breathtaking twist.

THE MYSTERIOUS AFFAIR AT STYLES

AGATHA CHRISTIE * 1920

This was Agatha Christie's first published novel, which she wrote during the First World War. She was partly inspired by her time working as a nurse ministering to Belgian soldiers to create her famous moustachioed character of Hercule Poirot. This tale of mystery is narrated by Arthur Hastings, a soldier on leave who is staying at the country manor house of Emily Inglethorp, an elderly wealthy woman who is discovered dead after being poisoned with strychnine. Hastings enlists the help of his friend Poirot, who delicately works alongside investigating officer Inspector Japp. There is a large number of suspects at Styles Court who all have secrets that they're desperate to conceal, but they are no match for Poirot, who always stays one step ahead of them – and us. The end includes a wickedly clever twist and establishes Poirot as a first-rate detective who cannot be fooled by red herrings.

Agatha Christie brilliantly describes her Belgian hero's cunning ability to carefully analyse seemingly insignificant facts. It's impressive how fully formed he appears from the beginning, and it's no wonder he became one of the world's most beloved detectives appearing in thirty-three novels and more than fifty short stories.

FAVOURITE READS

★

★

★

★

★

★

★

★

★

★

★

★

★

★

★

★

★

★

TBR PILE

★

★

★

★

★

★

★

★

★

★ _____

★ _____

★ _____

★ _____

★ _____

★ _____

★ _____

★ _____

★ _____

THOUGHTS

INDEX

Published in 2022 by Murdoch Books, an imprint of Allen & Unwin

Murdoch Books UK
Ormond House
26–27 Boswell Street
London WC1N 3JZ
Phone: +44 (0) 20 8785 5995
murdochbooks.co.uk
info@murdochbooks.co.uk

Murdoch Books Australia
83 Alexander Street
Crows Nest NSW 2065
Phone: +61 (0)2 8425 0100
murdochbooks.com.au
info@murdochbooks.com.au

For corporate orders and custom publishing, contact our business
development team at salesenquiries@murdochbooks.com.au

Publisher: Céline Hughes
Designer: Madeleine Kane
Production Director: Niccolò De Bianchi

ISBN 978 1 92261 647 0

A catalogue record for this book is available from the British Library

A catalogue record for this
book is available from the
National Library of Australia

Colour reproduction by Born Group, London, UK
Printed by Print Best, Estonia

10 9 8 7 6 5 4 3 2 1